DESIGN
and decorate
BATHROOMS

Lesley Taylor

Adams Media Corporation
Holbrook, Massachusetts

To my husband Kevin for all his support and encouragement.

This edition published by Adams Media Corporation
260 Center Street
Holbrook, MA 02343
by arrangement with New Holland (Publishers) Ltd.

ISBN 1-55850-750-7 (pbk)

A B C D E F G H I J
CIP information available upon request from the publisher.

Managing Editor: Coral Walker
Special photography: Janine Hosegood
Designed by: Grahame Dudley Associates
Editor: Emma Callery
Illustrator: Madeleine Floyd

Printed and bound in Malaysia

Contents

Introduction

We can all have hours of pleasure designing and decorating our homes. The choosing of colors and decorative products, the application and installation and, finally, the reality of a well planned room, is a very rewarding process. Provided, that is, that the result is pleasing and practical.

Decorating a bathroom can take a lot of planning. The products must not only work together to give you your chosen look, but they must also be practical. What is the use of an aesthetically pleasing bathroom that doesn't allow you the leg room to use the toilet, or where the wallpaper starts to peel off the walls within days of decorating?

Whether you want to start from scratch or just give your room a quick makeover, *Design and Decorate Bathrooms* is designed to take you through the maze of products that are now available. It gives you advice on planning and layout, and lets you know what sort of decorative finishes are most suitable for use in a bathroom. It has sections on storage and gives space-saving ideas. Window treatments are also discussed together with the most popular wall and floor finishes.

In the Style File section, there is a wide range of decorative styles of bathroom, and I give you advice on the elements that create each particular look. So, whether you wish to create a country house bathroom that is formal and elegant or your own Mediterranean retreat, you can achieve it with the help of *Design and Decorate Bathrooms*. Happy decorating.

Layout *and* planning

If you are removing an old bathroom, or designing a new one, planning is essential to success. It not only ensures a pleasant looking room, but also one that works. Before you consider the decorative style of your bathroom you should work out the most successful layout. Only by exploring the various options available can you hope to create a room that makes the most of the space given. The best way to ensure that you have got it right is to plan it on paper first.

Simply draw out your room to scale on graph paper. Use every square inch on the graph to represent a unit of distance in your room. For example, 1:20 scale means that 1 inch on your scaled drawing represents 20 inches in your room, and so on. Simple.

Measure your room using a tape measure, and ensure that you include information like the electrical outlets and plumbing, if relevant, on the plan. Certain rules of thumb apply: existing exterior plumbing, such as the waste pipe cannot be moved easily, so you will need to bear this in mind. Moldings and decorative tile work should also be considered.

Once you have drawn the outline of your room, draw templates of the various items that will be fitted, e.g., the bath, toilet, and sink, using a ruler and a T-square, if necessary. Use the same scale as the floor plan. It is very easy to find measurements for these items, as most brochures will have a technical section displaying this information.

FREESTANDING
Most modern sinks have been designed to be pleasing to the eye as well as functional. Pipework is kept to a minimum and integrated into the overall design.

If your room has sloping ceilings or any unusual features that may affect the layout of the bathroom, then those areas affected should also be drawn to scale on a separate piece of graph paper. This is known as an elevation, and will help you to determine whether an item will fit comfortably into the space available. To achieve this, you will need to draw the fixtures to scale, showing their height and width, as opposed to the length and width, as required for the floor plan.

Once this is complete, carefully cut out the fixtures. You can then move them around on the floor plan, trying them on the elevations if needed, until you find the best layout for the room.

Remember to allow for the opening of doors and windows, and also take leg room into consideration around toilets. Generally, 24 inches is sufficient. Allow 28 inches in front of the shower or bath to enable you to get in and out comfortably, and 28 inches in front of a sink to enable you to bend over to wash, with an additional 6 inches elbow room on either side.

Once you think you may have found the best layout, draw the fixtures onto your floor plan and elevation and you can then plan any additional storage and shelving. If you are considering the addition of a chest of drawers, make sure you have enough available space for the drawers to open.

I always find it best to then leave the plans for a day or two

SPACE SHAVING
Traditional shaving mirrors look smart, adjust to various positions and fold back for more space.

ROOM TO PLAN
A large bathroom needs as much thought as a small one. This room can accommodate several other fixtures – a bidet or shower, for example – with ease.

and review them with a fresh eye to see if anything has been missed. You may also decide at this point to add additional features such as a raised floor area (great for hiding pipework) or a small partition wall, for example.

To give you an idea of what you can do, look at the plans below. They are all possible alternatives to the room opposite.

ALTERED STATES

The plans are all based on the bathroom opposite without major plumbing alterations. The exterior wall (for the waste) is the one at the base of each plan.

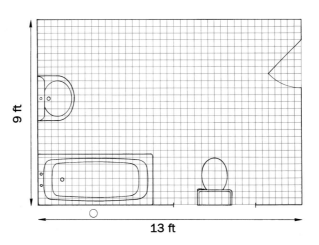

9 ft

13 ft

◀ The plan illustrated is of the bathroom opposite. Although spacious, you can see there is plenty of room for alterations (see below).

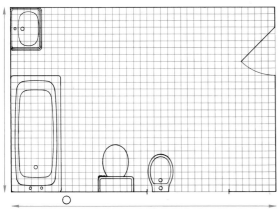

The sink has been moved to the end of the bath (plumbing can run underneath the bath. A bidet has been put next to the toilet.

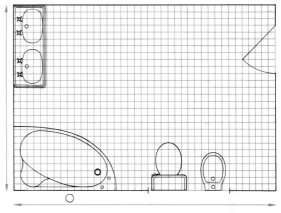

A corner bath takes up less space allowing for a double vanity unit to be fitted.

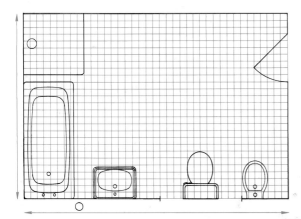

With the main fixtures all sitting on the exterior wall, there is room for a shower cubicle in the corner.

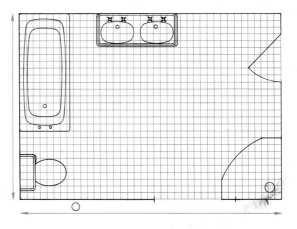

Plumbing for the vanity unit can be run along the wall and under the bath. A corner shower fits on the exterior wall.

STYLE *file*

A bathroom is the one place in the house where you can truly unwind after a stressful day and it is also a private place where you can pamper yourself – which is why the atmosphere created by the way you decorate the space is so important. Ultimately, it should be practical, welcoming, warm and a room in which you feel totally relaxed.

Bathrooms, like kitchens, can be expensive if you are starting from scratch, so it is important to get the layout right. But even if you are looking to make over your existing bathroom, once you decide to decorate, it is worth choosing a style or theme to follow.

A bathroom can be bright and sunny: a room to lift your spirits on the coldest of mornings, or it can be classically chic, using cool granite and marble. There is now an ever-increasing range of decorative products on the market, from ceramic tiles and clear plastic panelling to solid vinyl wallcoverings and mildew-resistant paints, giving you virtually unlimited choice when styling your bathroom.

So how do you decide on your style? You may wish to reproduce a room that is in keeping with the period of the house. Art deco

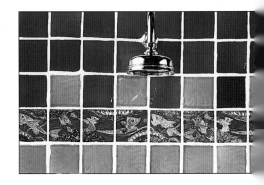

glamor from the 1930s, perhaps, or a half-timbered country cottage or elegant Georgian-style townhouse. The choice is yours.

TOP LEFT
This stunning bathroom uses marble and granite finishes to great effect. A polished wood mirror frame provides a much-needed touch of warmth.

BOTTOM LEFT
The ultimate fantasy bathroom: skilful trompe l'oeil transforms plain walls into a classical landscape.

TOP RIGHT
Blue and cream are traditional nautical colors and here the theme has been followed by an oar serving as a novel curtain rod.

BOTTOM RIGHT
This bathroom offers a taste of stylish Hollywood splendor, using mosaics, marble, mirrors and chrome.

Traditional style

Traditional bathrooms are those which include an element or theme derived from the past. This does not mean, however, that they have to be decorated in a pure form of a particular period. Elements of Georgian styling can successfully be mixed with Victorian ceramics to give the room an individual, yet still traditional, feel. Recently, this style of bathroom has become very popular with many manufacturers making period-style fixtures. These can be teamed with all manner of decorative items to enhance this nostalgic theme.

Many archive fabrics and wall coverings are now being reprinted in their original colors to fill the demand for this traditional style. Care must be taken when choosing traditional wall coverings and paints, as those made in the original way may

TRICKERY

▲ Prior to the mass production of wallpaper, trompe l'oeil, a hand-painted form of decoration designed to trick the eye, was very popular together with stencilling for adding decoration to a wall. This traditionally-styled bathroom has used this form of decoration to create the illusion of draped fabric.

VICTORIAN SPLENDOR

▶ Ceramic tiles to dado level and the heavy floral wallpaper above give this room its traditional atmosphere.

not be suitable for use in a modern bathroom, where steam and moisture can cause problems. Whenever possible, use a vinyl-based paint and wall covering.

DIVISIONS
Dividing the walls with dado and picture rails reduces the appearance of high ceilings.

A warm ocher and
period pieces evoke

This bathroom has both character and warmth. Elements such as the clawfoot tub and the chrome, wall-mounted shower head add a traditional air to the room, while the terracotta floor and the carefully chosen paint colors give it a warm, almost provincial, feel. The muted tones enhance the room's restful appearance, something that brighter, sunny colors would not achieve.

If this room were to be left undecorated, with the exception of the arched window and the beamed ceilings, it would have very little character. But it is the carefully chosen items that add to the atmosphere here, backed up by the cleverly selected paint colors. Increasingly, paint manufacturers are producing historic color paints in forms that are suitable for the bathroom. Latex paint, for example, is a washable and hard-wearing, water-based paint that can be used on all plaster walls and ceilings. Oil paint is even more durable, but more difficult to clean up after using it. In addition, it can be difficult to dispose of safely.

A hand-carved wooden pedestal houses the white sink (opposite), around which there is a collection of accessories: an old pine towel rail, a pretty scrolled shelf with its lace cloth, a traditional mirror, pictures, and a delicate, fluted glass wall sconce. All of these have been chosen for their traditional qualities. They are all personally collected items, and therefore add a unique quality to the room.

The attractive, slightly arched, window has no curtains, but a sheer screen is available,

MAKING IT YOUR OWN
A collection of antique paraphernalia or *bric-à-brac* can add more personality and character to a room than the most carefully chosen wallpapers or fabrics.

old-fashioned elegance

should it be needed. The fine fabric would provide privacy without blocking out any light or making the room look crowded.

The room has a particularly high ceiling, but the beams have been stained in a dark color in an attempt to visually lower its height. This technique also successfully draws attention to the beams as a feature of the bathroom.

GROUND LEVEL
Natural terracotta flooring adds a softness and warmth to a room in a way that no other form of ceramic tiling can.

A special retreat with
sheer fabric and golden

This cream bathroom has been decorated using some clever, yet simple, techniques. The main body of the room has been painted in a rich cream paint, as has the pipework and tank of the toilet. This helps them blend into the background of the room, allowing other features to become more prominent, especially the gold cherubs and sun that have been decoupaged on

SIMPLY ELEGANT

This bathroom is basically rather simple and would be very dull if just painted and tiled. Instead, a few chosen elements – the curtain, light fixture, candle holders and dramatic bath canopy – create a great impact on the finished room.

angels

the wall and toilet tank. Decoupage is a very simple process – choose a paper design or illustration, cut it out and stick to the surface using the correct adhesive, and then varnish it several times to give a hard-wearing surface. This last step is especially important in a bathroom as it also prevents the paper from peeling off with the large amounts of condensation that tend to occur, particularly if the room is a small one.

A practical, wood lookalike, vinyl floor covering has been chosen, which is a good alternative to natural wood flooring in the bathroom because there is always the danger of water leakage, and permanent damage may be done to a wooden floor. Another suitable flooring would be sealed cork tiles, which have the advantage of being warm underfoot.

The white clawfoot tub has been dramatically dressed using a sheer canopy attached to a decorative brass rod protruding from the wall above the bath. This is just a traditional curtain rod that has been attached using a specially designed wall bracket. If you are considering a similar bath canopy, choose a synthetic fabric rather than cotton, which may become stained by moisture. Try something similar with a shower curtain.

The window has been dressed using a striking, black on cream Corinthian-style panel, which is simply threaded onto a curtain rod. A panel like this should have just a slight fullness, to add softness, but not so much that the outline of the pattern becomes lost when the curtain is drawn.

TRADITIONAL DETAILS
▲ This reproduction faucet and shower set would add grace to any traditional bathroom. Most period-style fixtures are now readily available, everything from chrome-plated Art Deco to pretty brass Victorian-style models.

SHOWER PROOF
▼ There is a wide choice of curtains available for showers. Here the cherubs link it neatly with the angels-decoupage and they are complemented by the cream tassels.

Contemporary style

Bathroom designs that fall under the heading "contemporary," are some of my favorites. Contemporary styles can be as simple or detailed as you like. They can emulate a current trend or be designed in a very personal way, incorporating items that give you great personal pleasure.

Contemporary fixtures are continually being developed, ranging from whirlpool baths and showers with variable pulsating sprays to the most streamlined of sinks and faucets. This means that the parameters within which the designer can work are very wide, resulting in some truly imaginative bathrooms.

COLOR CONFIDENT

In this stylish, modern bathroom, clean lines and muted shades of green and red are brought to life with the addition of the yellow shelving. A storage unit like this should be built into the basic shower/bath housing. But if that is impossible, a simple shelf, painted in a vibrant color, as here, would solve storage problems and add contrast.

PERSONAL PLEASURES

▼ This very modern bathroom suite has been teamed with a montage of colorful ceramic tiles and Moroccan-influenced accessories to create a haven for the bather.

CONTINENTAL CHIC

◀ Floor-to-ceiling ceramic tiles add a European feel to this bathroom. They are strikingly modern, yet create a warm and comfortable note with their tortoiseshell colors.

Seashore style using
shades of

Seashore and nautical themes have become a great form of inspiration for designers in recent years. The memories of a childhood seaside holiday, and the freshness of the clear blue sea, can easily be captured within the design of a room. There is a great number of blue shades from which to choose, so search out the particular color that you would most like in your room.

As with most bathrooms, storage plays a very important role, and there is ample storage here, but it has been decorated to

COLOR CHOICE
▼ Both color and texture play their part in this room. The blue of the sea and sky, warm gold from the sand, and the clean white of the clouds on a sunny day are combined with the smooth texture of sun-bleached timbers that have been washed up on the shore.

ocean blue

blend into the overall scheme, as opposed to being used as a feature. It is not difficult to unify cabinets with their surroundings and create a complete look; here, the decorator has used paint finishes that are complementary to the colorwash chosen to decorate the walls below the dado. Part of the secret to a well-designed themed room is the ability to adapt or disguise the principal elements needed to furnish that room. By doing this, you will find that they look comfortable within the chosen theme, adding to the overall effect of the room rather than detracting from it.

Many modern bathrooms are now built without the benefit of a window. Not only does this mean that you are reliant on artificial lighting but it can also have the psychological effect of looking claustrophobic, regardless of how large the room is. One answer to this would be to create a false window, as shown here. Cleverly, wooden shutters have been built into a frame resembling a window opening. The whole has then been dressed using a sheer muslin curtain and some accessories added to make even more of a feature.

There are various ways to create a false window, and one of my particular favorites is a trompe l'oeil painting of a window with its view beyond. You could create the vista of your dreams; maybe the Hanging Gardens of Babylon, a rush hour in Manhattan, or a beautiful bay with golden sands.

DECORATIVE DETAILS
Accessories play a very important part in a themed room like this. The sea horse and fish opposite, for example, are small ceramic shapes that can be stuck to plain tiles to provide textural interest.

STARTING OFF
▼ A handful of shells may be a good starting point if redecorating your family bathroom. This border has been made by stamping the motifs onto plain paper, a delightfully simple way to coordinate a theme.

A monochromatic scheme
using rich cream

Lighting is what makes the design of this mainly cream bathroom so successful, as low-voltage halogen lights have been chosen to give a pure white light. With traditional lighting, the room would have taken on a duller, yellowish appearance.

The fixtures are in a traditional style and, to enhance this, the bath and pipework have been concealed within panelled boxing. The space above the bath has also been boxed in to create a recessed bath and shower area, and conceal the wiring for the lighting. To make the boxing look like an existing detail and to neaten the effect, the coving has been continued in front of the partitioning.

Most bathrooms will have areas that can be aesthetically improved with some form of boxing. Pipes running behind the fixtures in the room are unsightly and can be hidden behind timber housing. This can then either be painted, as here, tiled or wallpapered. Remember, however, to allow an access panel for maintenance of the pipes. It is also worth considering the height of the boxing, as it could make a handy shelf. This sort of work is comparatively simple if you are handy with a saw, hammer and nails. But if in doubt, ask a local carpenter to do the work for you: it can be done quickly and easily.

A few decorative additions quietly give a lift to this

FINISHING TOUCHES
Bathroom accessories chosen for their interesting shape or form work well in a simple bathroom.

gives classic appeal

bathroom. The walnut lookalike floor adds warmth and its attractiveness is increased by the inset, mahogany-colored border. The carefully chosen footstool helps to draw out the border, making it a more prominent feature. A pair of mono-chrome prints, positioned opposite each other at either side of the bath, also bring a little extra tonal relief and pattern to the

TONE AND DETAIL

The paintings or prints hanging in your rooms have a great impact on the finished atmos-phere. These are things that should be chosen with great care, and if you can't find what you are looking for, have something commis-sioned – it is not always as expensive as you would imagine, espe-cially if you try the local art schools.

Aquamarine provides a
sense of space and

COMBINING COLORS

Cool colors like aquamarine can produce a welcoming room when teamed with warm colors from the color spectrum such as yellows, golds and oranges.

Aquamarine is very restful and calming, and while it is classed as a cool color, when teamed with one from the opposite side of the spectrum, it can be used to produce a relaxing room that is far warmer in atmosphere than if used by itself.

This bathroom is just such an example. The walls are tiled to dado height in a softly mottled, aquamarine ceramic. This offers an attractive and practical surface, above which tongue and groove panelling has been applied. It has been colorwashed in a different tone than the ceramic tiles, adding interest to the fin-

f r e s h n e s s

ished room. The remainder of the walls have been painted in a matte-finish blue-green in a deeper tone. To add further airiness, simple white cotton curtains have been used as a decorative feature at the far end of the room.

Tongue and groove panelling is very popular in bathrooms as it is easy to install and can be painted with any type of effect, or stained, varnished or waxed. It is also useful for boxing in unsightly areas. Usually it extends from floor to dado height, so this particular bathroom illustrates a very different effect that can be created with tongue and groove. You don't have to buy individual strips as it is now available in molded panels. If you can't install it yourself, ask a carpenter to do it.

Warm colors and tones have been introduced into the lower half of this bathroom, via the mellow wood in the vanity unit and the panelling around the bath. More of the gold is used for the natural floor matting, ensuring that the ratio of warm, mellow gold to aquamarine is evenly matched within the room. The checked bath mat cleverly unites the two principal colors.

The balance of two colors can dramatically change the appearance of a finished room. Take the one here, for example. If the golden flooring was replaced by a deep aquamarine carpet, the result would be more formal, unlike the warm, welcoming atmosphere, seen here. This is because the gold in the wood would only appear as an accent color and not as an integral part of the color scheme.

WARMTH AND CONTRAST

▲ Golden accessories and decorative details are used here to introduce warmth and contrast to this white and aquamarine bathroom.

COLORFUL RUGS

▼ Cotton dhurries are widely available in a myriad colors. This makes them very useful if you want to add a spot of color to a bathroom. They are also cheap to purchase – always an attractive proposition.

Cottage & Country

Cottage rooms tend to fall into two categories, or are a mixture of the two. They are feminine and pretty, or textured, with a homespun feel. Full-blown roses and country checks work well in both styles, as do beamed ceilings and small, leaded windows.

While the pretty country cottage bathroom contains chintz fabrics and coordinating, patterned wallpapers and borders, the more textured room has exposed stonework with roughly plastered or limewashed walls, flagstone floors or a textured natural matting. These rooms look good with plain cotton furnishings and old-style stencil designs and distressed paint finishes.

Country rooms, however, have a slightly grander appearance, sometimes with larger rooms incorporating formal features such as Georgian sash windows. They can also be home to chintzes and frills on furnishings and elaborate window dressings.

FLORAL FANTASY
Lemon and green are harmonious colors which, when united in coordinating wallpaper, borders and ceramic tiles, create the perfect cottage room. The effect has been further enhanced by the choice of design – small sprig prints are very reminiscent of cottage style.

HIGH SHELVING
▼ The shelf at picture rail height strikes the right note for a country bathroom, especially with a display of plates.

ROSE-TINTED
◄ This rather ordinary bathroom has been given the country touch with blowsy roses and lace-edged curtains.

Country look
without fuss

Toile de Jouy is a style of fabric originally produced in the town of Jouy, in France. The technique came into production after 1770, following the invention of a copper plate printing machine that permitted large, but delicately drawn patterns to be printed in a single process. Fabric designs were then developed, depicting people and animals that told a story of, for example, an opera, a contemporary event, or a mythological subject. These fabrics became extremely popular and were subsequently produced in many regions of France.

Today, fabrics and wall coverings in the style of toile de Jouy are enjoying a revival. The designs are very elegant, and instantly add a delicate, traditional air to a room. If you want to achieve a country look simply and easily, these are the designs to look for. They are both pretty and sophisticated and tone in well with any existing bathroom suite. The nicely proportioned bathroom featured opposite illustrates just how effective toile de Jouy can be. The white tiles used as a backsplash behind the sink and around the bath have prevented the pattern from becoming too overwhelming.

A complementary fabric has been used to dress the window and upholster the small Louis-style chair next to the sink. This fabric works well with the wallpaper

SMALL THINGS
▲ Wall-mounted shelving offers the perfect chance to display your favorite collectibles, while adding character to a room. Lace edging such as this is especially suitable for a cottage-style bathroom.

TOILE DE JOUY
◄ This style of fabric and wall coverings adds a romantic elegance to a country scheme.

using toile de Jouy

because it is the same color. But, more importantly, it is on a smaller, more compact scale, which contrasts with the flowing, open design of the toile de Jouy.

The aquamarine print on the wallpaper and fabric is lifted by the introduction of the warm, caramel flooring. This gives the room a welcoming glow that is sometimes missing in a room decorated using cool colors. The gilt mirrors and picture frames have the same effect and also add a slightly opulent feel to the room, synonymous with the period in which the wallpaper was originally designed.

SMALL SCALE DESIGNS
Reproductions of both traditional wallpapers and fabrics add a nostalgic air to a room.

Country elegance:
crimson, dark wood and

Creating an individual bathroom that includes as much of your personality as possible, while producing a scheme that is sympathetic to the age of the property, can be difficult. This bathroom, however, manages to achieve just that balance. The owner finds busy flowers and frills overpowering, yet wants to retain a traditional cottage feel to the room. The result is a striking blend of traditional colors, with an underlying oriental theme.

The inspiration for the decorative scheme in this bathroom has come from the collection of oriental-style plates, chosen to decorate the walls. The deep red in the plates has been picked

MAKE A FEATURE OF IT
Accessories like plates are a simple way to decorate a plain wall, and can have as much impact on a room as patterned wallpaper.

a gallery of plates

out for the soft furnishings and some of the paintwork. The red adds life to the mainly black and white beamed room, and visually helps to reduce the ceiling height by being used above the picture rail.

It is not difficult to add a picture rail to a wall. Likewise, mock beams are also readily available to add to walls and ceilings and can work especially well in an older type of property.

The white, traditional bathroom suite, with its simple lines and chrome shower and mixer faucets, is the perfect option for a room like this one. Furthermore, by decorating the bath panel with a mahogany colored woodstain to match the ceiling and soft furnishings, this potentially dominating feature is drawn into the overall decor of the room.

Soft furnishings are kept simple, with detailing coming from the pattern of the fabric as opposed to the style of curtaining. The design of the fabric shows various traditional sailing vessels, including one of oriental design, and is printed on a rich, cream background. Many people would be concerned using a fabric with a cream base in a room with white walls. But, as you can see, cream can work very well, adding warmth to the overall scheme and softening the hardness of the blocks of black, white and red. These colors are also used in the kilim rug, enhancing the unity still further.

HANGING PLATES

◀ Different types of plate hanging devices are available depending on whether you want to hang plates separately or group them together, as shown here.

RED AND WHITE

▲ Many people think of red and white as a very modern combination, but, in fact, it is as traditional as blue and white, and can add a nostalgic warmth to any room.

Mediterranean look

Mediterranean-style interiors have become extremely popular in recent years and it is not difficult to gain inspiration for a room in this genre. A quick flick through travel brochures will soon give you plenty of ideas for ways in which to recreate the warm sand, yellow sunshine, deep blue seas and the bold pattern and rich artifacts specific to that particular setting.

One of the nicest things about this style of decor is the variety of different cultures that come under its banner. Various influences range from those of southern Spain, with its colorful ceramics, whitewashed houses and citrus fruits; to the cultures of north Africa with their terracotta walls, richly colored textiles and beautiful copper and brass trinkets. Each country offers a warm and rich style of its own.

CONTRASTING COLORS

Citrus green walls and small mosaic tiles are the perfect backdrop against which to bathe. The deep blue base molding and towels are a strong accent color, throwing the green into relief.

COLONNADED SPLENDOR

▲ If the texture and colors of the Mediterranean isn't good enough, then transform your bathroom into a classical landscape with the use of trompe l'oeil.

EARTH COLORS

◄ Terracotta flooring and colorwashed walls in glorious sun-drenched yellow capture the earthy warmth of the Mediterranean. Rustic accessories add character, while the large sunflowers are typical of the region.

Tranquil effects
with relaxing

Color has a great impact on the atmosphere of a room and here the cooler colors are used to create a relaxing and very stylish room full of character and detail.

The walls are softly colorwashed in aquamarine, a color which is then used in careful solid blocks in the accessories. Accent color – here it is shades of yellow – is added to bring subtle contrast to the room, with the carved bird at the foot of the bath, the sponge, bath salts and the lilies. This is a subtle way to bring the room alive.

The clawfoot tub takes centre stage on a raised floor area, which not only divides the bathroom area from the rest of the room but also conceals any pipework. Sitting aloft as it does, the tub merits some decoration and here a humorous fish motif painted on the side does just that. The motif is echoed in a slightly different form stencilled at picture rail level; this helps to bring the eyeline down from the high ceiling and further enhances the room's sense of unity.

Glass blocks have been used instead of panes of glass, giving privacy yet ample light and retaining the simple, clean lines of the room. There are many different types of glass block available; in addition to the ones featured opposite, you can also buy different textures and colors. The mellow timber floor adds a little warmth without detracting from the overall relaxing effect of the color scheme.

colors

Finally, chrome has been chosen for the faucets, towel bar and occasional tables, enhancing the stylized and modern theme. Often, you will find that non-colors (black, white) and various metals, will provide the perfect foil to any color scheme. They add interest but at the same time don't detract from the overall effect that you have so carefully planned.

ACCESSORIZE
Color and texture introduced in accessories add character to any room. Green glass and coordinating towels are not expensive yet may be all you need to transform a plain room.

Mediterranean textures
with a north African

It is quite obvious where the designer gained inspiration for this wonderfully unusual bathroom, and the way in which she has chosen to use elements reminiscent of the northern regions of Africa is very refreshing.

The shower curtain with its African animals is a great choice for a room with this theme and is a good focal point. Shower curtains are available in a diverse range, but if you have difficulty finding one with a suitable pattern, buy a transparent one and back it with some cotton fabric of your choice. Attach the cotton to the top of the shower curtain so it can be removed for regular laundering.

The waterproof sand and cement covered walls are a very novel and effective way of introducing texture. If you are looking for a speedy make over and have no need to replaster the walls, you could achieve a similar effect with a textured masonry paint. This is impervious to water and the finish is especially useful for covering badly cracked or unattractive walls.

The white bathroom suite is an ideal foil for most schemes. Here, it is important to the appearance of the finished room as it adds a crisp contrast of color next to the predominance of gold. The white makes the gold appear richer, and hence the white looks brighter. The brass faucets and shower fixtures with their white details ensure that the suite is harmonious with its environment.

THE THIRD DIMENSION
◄ Intaglio designs can be incorporated into your textured wall. Make small templates from thick card. Apply a layer of petroleum jelly to the back of the templates and pin them to the wall. Apply the finish or paint and leave to dry before removing.

touch

A heavily woven natural floor covering has been used, once again a product that is very much at home in this themed bathroom. The finishing touches – the rustic metal mirror frame and the bamboo cane with its straw finial for the shower curtain rod – are witty assets to this room.

THEMATIC ACCESSORIES

▲ Shower curtain rods do not hold a lot of weight so they can be made from any number of materials. This bamboo cane offers the ideal alternative. Copper tubing and a raffia brush complete the effect with an African-style finial.

IN THE HEAT OF THE DAY

◄ The rough covered walls in a rich caramel color can be finished with a masonry sealant for extra waterproofing.

Almost white

Despite the wide range of colored bathroom fixtures, white still remains the most popular, owing no doubt to its great adaptabil-

ity. If you are lucky enough to have inherited a white bathroom suite from the previous householder, it is worth leaving it intact and decorating the bathroom around it.

WARM WOOD
◀ This very practical room, covered from top to bottom in ceramic tiles, has been given a more domestic air by the introduction of the wooden table and its accessories.

The white bathroom is rather like a chameleon, altering its appearance depending on its surroundings: it can be elegant and feminine, bold and modern, or cool and clinical. White bathrooms need not be limited to white alone. In some schemes, other colors are very successfully included.

Many people find the thought of a white bathroom suite teamed with both white tiles and walls rather cold, but the introduction of various other elements and textures to the room, can make it very pleasing indeed. Take the bathroom, opposite top, for example. Although ostensibly a white room, the addition of colorful accessories, like the blue tieback and the starfish picture, detract from what could be a rather clinical space. The softening effect of the sheer curtain hanging down to floor level, the large bunch of flowers and the profusion of bottles on the glass shelf go further towards making this a very lived-in room. The other examples on this page and overleaf on pages 40-45 will give you many different suggestions for ways to adapt a white bathroom to suit your style.

BLACK AND WHITE
▼ White, black and chrome work together extremely well to produce a more masculine, yet opulent, bathroom.

MODERN SIMPLICITY
◀ This chic bathroom includes up-to-the minute styling supplied by the sink set into a tinted glass and cast-iron shelf.

Marble and glass offset
the clean look

When decorating a room, the designer has a number of options, one of which is whether to decorate using color and pattern or with design detail and texture. The cosmopolitan bathroom below definitely falls into the latter category. It is far more difficult to design in this way; the decorator is completely reliant on an eye for detail as opposed to the impact that pattern and color can have on a room.

Structurally, this room has a number of interesting details, such as the sloping walls and the skylight (seen here reflected in

MIRROR MIRROR
Clever design details and the use of mirrors help to enhance all the best features in this room, while disguising its size.

of all-white

the mirror), but proportionately, it is quite small. The designer has drawn attention to its good features, while disguising the poor ones.

The skylight is central to the ceiling, and to add detail to the area, a simple run of coving has been attached to frame it. As a further design detail, the perimeter of the ceiling has been given an attractive molding which also serves to house the wiring for the low-voltage halogen lighting. This form of lighting is of great importance in a white color scheme as it produces a pure white light.

A white marble with a distinctive grey vein has been chosen to cover both the walls and floor. Marble is a very versatile product as it can be cut in various thicknesses to be used on both of these surfaces, and to create vanity and bath tops and panels. Faux marble tiles are a cheaper alternative to the real thing.

The lines of the room are clean and simple, and to enhance this, the shower cubicle has been built at the furthest end of the bathroom, partly concealed behind a marble and mirror clad partition. A ventilation panel has been included to alleviate condensation problems within the shower. The opposite wall, housing the entrance door, has also been mirrored, so that the room appears to be many times larger than it is in reality.

PLAIN AND SIMPLE
◀ When white, chrome, marble and gray-tinted glass tiles are combined they create a clean-lined, modern look.

A touch of gray adds *softness to a*

I think we all have our favorite styles of room: a romantic bedroom, and a comfortable family kitchen are certainly two of mine. When it comes to the bathroom, regardless of the style of decorating one chooses, for it to work successfully as a well-designed room, it should always look crisp and clean. A mainly white color scheme will nearly always offer that feel. The secret is to retain that quality while avoiding a clinical atmosphere.

The bathroom featured here has managed to achieve just that: it is a family bathroom that is both comfortable and fresh. White ceramic floor tiles provide an easy-to-clean surface that will not deteriorate with constant wear from wet feet. Being white, the tiles also give the illusion of maximizing space. Very simply decorated white ceramic tiles are also used around the bath and sink. This light-handed approach is easy on the eye and offers the most flexibility when it comes to redecorating the room, as introducing a new choice of wall covering and window treatment can give the room a completely new look.

The built-in shower ensures the lines of the room remain simple, which is especially important in a room this narrow. The simplicity of lines is also echoed by the window treatment. Practical, white painted shutters in a versatile design give the user various options, as the lower shutters can remain closed, obscuring the view, while the upper one opens for maximum light.

PAINTED DETAIL
◀ Plain white ceramic tiles are comparatively cheap to buy and can be easily decorated with cold ceramic paint. But bear in mind that this paint will not stand up to a lot of wear and tear so it is not suitable for areas such as showers and backsplashes.

whiter-than-white scheme

LIGHT AND FRESH
◀ The freshness of white gives light and vitality to a small bathroom.

NEUTRAL SHADES
▼ Small objects can add so much to a color scheme. Cream and brown blends surprisingly well with a white bathroom, softening a crisp effect.

The simple striped, gray-blue wallpaper softens the walls, especially on the left wall where it adds tonal contrast to the tiled walls and floor. The bathroom contains everything you would need, with toiletries within easy access. The pine picture frame and wooden, mahogany and brass accessories like the bath and sink faucets and the shaving brush on the shelf above the sink add a little warmth to the overall scheme.

A touch of glamor
with gold and

Those who think that wooden floor and walls should only be used in country schemes would benefit from seeing this bathroom. The wood panelling covers all areas of the walls and floors, with the exception of the built-in mirrored cabinets. The wood has been painted in a white gloss paint, giving a hard-wearing surface that also reflects light, making the room bright and airy.

The main bathroom is accessed via a dressing area, which is separated by a large archway. This houses mirror-fronted storage units and a large cane armchair; perfect for sitting on while you dry your toes.

The ceiling of both areas has been covered in a pretty candy-pink striped wallpaper and the stripes are also echoed on the wood panelling around the bath. Stylish though the ceiling may be, remember that wallpaper is not always practical in a bathroom as moisture can cause the paper to peel. As this particular bathroom is large, moisture is less likely to be a problem, but in a smaller room, ensure you have adequate ventilation to prevent excessive dampness.

The bath has some very glamorous, gold-plated fixtures, adding just a touch of luxury. Likewise, the light fitting is elaborate and elegant, the center light having pink crystals, the ideal link with the room.

Roman blinds dress the generous windows, their delicate pink and white fabric contrasting well with the candy striped ceiling. A scalloped edging softens their hard lines and a narrow,

WHITE WITH COLORS

If you want to recreate an almost white scheme but have colored bathroom fixtures and a low budget, paint the complete room white, including the ceiling and floorboards. Replace the bath panel with white painted wood and use white soft furnishings.

candy-stripe pink

pleated pink pelmet successfully punctuates the line where the walls meet the ceiling.

Finally, as in most well-designed rooms decorated in two colors, an accent color is supplied by the flourishing, deep green plants that are clearly extremely happy in this setting.

CANDY STRIPES

This white bathroom has pink and white stripes around the bath and on the ceiling, and the pink Roman blinds and pelmet. The pale tones add enormously to the room, making it into a very pretty and comfortable space.

Family bathrooms

Family bathrooms are, by definition, rooms that service the needs of each individual within a family. They should offer a safe and fun room for the kids, a room in which to preen and pamper for the self-conscious adolescent, and a place to relax and unwind for the hard-working parent. They should be practical and well-designed, offering ample storage for toiletries, and decorated using products made specifically for use in such an area of the home.

Safety should be of utmost importance in the family bathroom. Shiny marble floors, for example, may look wonderful, but would a busy ten-year-old think of putting down a towel before stepping wet-footed onto a potentially dangerous surface? And open shelves may be smart, but what about keeping pills away from inquisitive toddlers? These are just two examples of the differences that should be taken into consideration when decorating a family bathroom as opposed to any other.

CHECK IT OUT
Wallpaper instantly adds character. In this case, the chosen design is fun enough to appeal to the kids, yet smart enough for the grown-ups.

STORING IT ALL AWAY

▲ Bathroom cabinets, like kitchen cabinets, make the room so very practical and easy to clean. Ceramic tiles in bold primary colors and a range of sizes brighten what could be an otherwise plain room.

ALL CHANGE

◄ Painted wood-panelled walls are practical and versatile. The look of the room can be changed quite simply by redecorating using a different color palette.

Seashore medley teams
with deep azure

DRESSING UP

▲ Accessories can have a very strong presence in a room, changing both its character and atmosphere. Shells are wonderful decorative features and can be glued to wall panels, mirror frames or the edges of shelves.

CRISP AND CLEAN

▶ Ceramic tiles are one of the best form of decorative products you can use in a bathroom. There is a wide variety of designs available and the surface is practical, waterproof and easy to clean. These particular tiles have been stencilled with ceramic paint for a unique finish.

There is certainly plenty happening in this pretty blue and white bathroom. Once the coordinated color scheme was complete, seaside paraphernalia was used successfully to add decorative details.

Wallpapers in a blue and white stripe and a small bud design team beautifully with the blue and green floral border used to divide the walls at dado height. This type of color scheme has become very popular in recent years, with its coordinating fabrics and accessories. It creates a style that many find easy to live with as all the elements work together to produce a total look.

This room, however, also has a charmingly individual feel due to the choice of accessories. Sea horses and starfish sit happily beside flowing bouquets of pretty blue and green flowers. The mirror may once have been a simple sheet of glass, but it has been adorned with yet more starfish and many different types of shells to make something unique and also totally suitable for this bathroom. The bottles made of blue glass and the ceramic bowl and jug on the windowsill also add an individual flavor with the added bonus of toning-in beautifully with the color scheme. The whole room is reminiscent of a country cottage by the sea.

Many blue and white color schemes can appear cold, but the designer has counteracted this with the use of items in a mellow, golden color. The small pine shelf unit, table and

for a fun family room

**SHE SELLS
SEA SHELLS**
By mixing coordinated country cottage elements with seashore accessories, the designer of this room has succeeded in producing a very individual space.

blanket box, for example, together with the color introduced by the starfish, are attractive, warm contrasts to the basic blue and white scheme. The brass faucets and shower head have the same effect. A room that is decorated unremittingly in a single color, or with different tones of that color, can become dull. But with the injection of contrasting patches, the room is given a lift, successfully bringing it to life. Colors that work especially well with blue are yellow and pink.

Bright and beautiful
with raspberry, cherry

If your family is into contemporary styling, this bathroom may be for you. The colors are bright and inviting, but while they are vivid, they are not overpowering.

Simplicity is the key to this bathroom's success as the lines have been kept clean and sharp. The walls and bath panel are

CHILD'S PLAY
The children have taken a hand in accessorizing this colorful family bathroom. The painted paper plates are a cheap and extremely effective addition to a family bathroom. To prevent the designs from being spoiled by condensation, paint them with varnish that dries to a clear finish.

and orange

constructed from timber and incorporate recessed areas in which to display and store toys and toiletries. Note how all the toys are kept within a child's reach to be grabbed at bathtime. The glass bottles containing various perfumes and potions, however, are well out of reach further up the bathroom wall, as are the controls for the wall-mounted shower unit. Safety is quite rightly high on the agenda in this family bathroom.

It is always a good idea to decorate rooms for children, bearing in mind that they grow very quickly indeed, and as they grow, so their tastes change. So color schemes that work as a backdrop to toys and accessories have a longer life span than those incorporating fashionable characters or motifs. This bathroom is such an example. Children are made to feel this room is very much their own by the introduction of bathtime toys, and their own special artwork commissioned by mum and dad to decorate the walls. It is a good idea to ask a child to draw a special picture or, as here, decorate a paper plate to take pride of place on the wall. This type of accessory is also cheap and very effective, and once the child has grown, it can easily be replaced by a more recent piece.

DRYING OUT
▲ Turn your hand towels into a design feature by hanging them from a fun peg rack.

HAND PRINTS
◀ Children's hand prints are very charming and are a remarkably quick way to decorate paper plates such as those featured in the bathroom opposite.

Fresh pink check accents
a simple white

This is very much a country-style family bathroom. It is pretty, fresh, and fun. The main walls have been given a traditional beamed effect, reminiscent of old country properties, and the woodwork has been painted white to contrast with the powder blue walls.

Simply painted white boards offer a practical flooring, on which sit the white bathroom fixtures. In the center of the room is the very impressive tub. Simple in itself, once boxed in with tongue and groove wood panels, surrounded by a four-poster effect canopy and draped with pink checked curtains, it becomes the central feature of the room. This is a technique often employed by designers. By drawing attention to a central feature like this, and then decorating the surrounding room simply in an enhancing color, that feature dominates while the room remains uncluttered. In this way, the finished effect is special, but far from overpowering.

The light blue and white used here naturally make a room appear larger, and the small and simple accessories have been chosen for the room so as not to clutter up the space nor to detract from the central feature, the tub.

There are a number of ways to make the tub the main feature within the room. If plumbing permits, you can invest in a very elaborate, free-standing tub and

BRIGHT AND FRESH
▲ Gingham and check fabrics are very versatile. They work as well in a cottage room as they do in a simple country color scheme.

WICKER WORK
◀ Wicker chairs are simple and stylish. Bought new they are inexpensive, and old ones can be painted or color-rubbed. They fit in especially well with the practicality of a family bathroom.

and powder blue scheme

position it centrally in the room. Or, as here, use drapery tech-niques similar to those used over beds. Be aware, however, that the fabric used will need to be impervious to mildew and mois-ture, or suitable for regular laundering. As demonstrated in the picture above, the drapery doesn't have to be complicated to be effective. Indeed, if your tub is surrounded by three walls, one of the simplest ways to dress it would be to attach a shower cur-tain rod at ceiling height. Then, onto this, hang a pair of overly gathered curtains that can be held back using large tassel tiebacks. Stunning and simple – and very original, too

SIMPLICITY
▲ The simplicity of the decor in this bathroom makes it especially good for a family room. There is room to move about and clutter can be kept to a minimum.

Showers & powder rooms

Showers are more economical than baths, and in the time it takes to fill a tub, you could have already had a refreshing shower. There is also a lot of choice when it comes to shower fixtures. They are available as ready-made cubicles, or you can fit a shower unit into a custom-built space finished with an impervious surfacing material, such as ceramic tiles or marble.

Powder rooms normally consist of just a toilet and sink. Most homes with only an upstairs bathroom will find a ground floor powder room a very good investment, as not only does it avoid the constant wear and tear on furnishings as members of the family traipse up and down stairs, but it is generally accepted as adding extra value to your home.

COOL SURFACES
This chic shower room is clad in two colors of marble. Note how the shower has been cleverly built into the sloping ceiling of the room, using custom-made glass doors. It is making the most of a small space.

DECIDING FEATURES

▲ There are many interesting and beautifully designed bathroom fixtures available, which become a feature in themselves, setting the tone for the room.

WARM SHADES

◀ The custom-made shower can be as large as is practical, and, as you can see here, it can have a lot of character. There are six different colors of hand-made tile arranged randomly on each of the walls. Tiles like these have wonderful depths and variation of color because each one is carefully handglazed before firing.

The timeless appeal
of beige and white

Classic white is always an excellent base for a color scheme. Being a non-color, it works with any shade or hue you can think of. This means a room in which the permanent fixtures are all white can take on a totally different appearance, depending on the color or colors chosen to enhance it.

Here, a shower cubicle has been tiled from floor to ceiling

NATURE'S WAY
▲ Jute and cotton rope work well with accessories like the driftwood on the shelf next to the shower.

FABULOUS FABRIC
▶ For extra privacy in this shower cubicle, a monochromatic piece of fabric has been sandwiched between the two clear plastic panels in the door.

with a seascape theme

with white ceramic tiles, a detail of which are the diamond-shaped relief decor tiles. They give the area design detail and textural interest without the use of color. The surrounding walls, built-in shelved areas and floor have also been given the white treatment, thereby allowing the accessories to set the tone of the room.

The owner has decided that natural tones would offer an up-to-the-minute look for this shower room, which is an option that works very well. A fine raffia blind hides the toiletries stored on the upper shelves, while leaving carefully chosen accessories in view to enhance the current theme of the room. Natural sea sponges, decorative pieces of driftwood, glass and delicate metalwork all combine to create a display that is full of unusual textures and natural shades.

The director's chair in pine with white canvas seating and back is not only a feature in the room but has been placed directly in front of the shower door. This makes it a usefully accessible resting place for towels and bathrobes.

The look is very contemporary, but once the natural look has had its day, imagine how simple it will be to change the accessories and blinds, and achieve a refreshing new style.

SHARP DESIGN
Mix cream and beige with seashore trophies and mementoes. Set against white ceramic, the overall effect is harmonious, yet has the cutting edge of good design.

Classic blue and white
creates a well-dressed

Many old houses do not have the benefit of a powder room, but if one is incorporated into the house at a later date, it should be decorated in an appropriate way. This powder room most certainly achieves this as blue and white is a classic combination, successfully standing the test of time.

Reproduction ceramic tiles have been used to decorate the lower wall areas of this generous room. They have been fitted

CLASSIC STYLE
Thanks to the use of blue and white, this elegant powder room has a clean and fresh atmosphere.

powder room

BLOWING BUBBLES

▶ A less conventional detail like this ceramic fish can be used very successfully in a classic setting as it provides a little light relief.

with a decorative molding in the same color as a feature at dado height, below which a deeper blue moulding has been inserted, echoing the same detail just above the base molding. This type of approach adds depth and design detail, but without introducing additional color which can be confusing in a room this size.

A traditional white toilet and sink have been chosen, no doubt to match the other similar, original fixtures within the house. Furthermore, the parquet flooring links into the hallway, another way of making a new room appear an original feature.

Paint is a very practical finish, especially in areas with moisture, and while decorative finishes are considered to be a modern trend, many, in fact, derive from an era prior to the mass production of wallpaper. Sponging is therefore a very serviceable and apt form of decoration for this room. In this particular room, a base color of white has been softly and evenly decorated with two tones of blue. This is a simple finish, which, if done correctly, looks very effective.

Accessories once again complete the required look. A collection of china and trinkets give the room a lived-in feel, and a carefully positioned rug draws in the generous floor area. The white muslin curtain and hand towel are beautifully fresh.

THE SMALLER THINGS

◀ Because white and blue is such a popular combination of colors, there are many accessories available to bring a classic powder room like this to life.

FOCUS *file*

When you begin to design a room, it is always a good idea to have an ultimate look or theme in mind. This makes choosing the practical and decorative elements that you need to include that much easier. If you are investing in new bathroom fixtures, it is all too easy to shop around and commit yourself to a certain style before considering the other main elements needed to complete the scheme. This can mean that you are forced into using a type of flooring or wallcovering that isn't exactly what you want because it is the only thing available to enhance that particular style of bathroom fixture.

In this section, I look at the principal elements: the flooring, wallcoverings, windows, and fixtures. These are all vital to the look of any room. If you have new bathroom "furniture," you will want to make it a feature. On the other hand, if you have inherited your bathroom, you may want to disguise the fixtures with decorative finishes and details.

The bathroom featured here is truly stunning as it is a good example of being both practical and smart. It is filled with very stylish pieces, which work together exceptionally well, bringing both texture and color to the room. The approach is simple as there are not too many conflicting finishes, and an emphasis has been placed on good design rather than pattern.

If you plan to redecorate a room in your home, don't be tempted to add all your existing accessories to the new color

NEW OR OLD?
Start with the bathroom "furniture." Do you want to work around the fixtures you have, or invest in new ones?

scheme – unless, of course, they really work well in it. A fluffy toilet seat cover would not be welcome in this particular bathroom, regardless of its color.

On the next few pages we look in detail at some of the elements you may need to consider when designing and decorating a bathroom such as walls, floors, windows and fixtures.

FEATURES
Consider architectural details like windows when deciding on a style for a room. The simple geometric lines of the window and the simple shape of this bathroom were the basis for its final look.

Walls *and* floors

Wall and floor finishes need careful consideration in a bathroom, more so than many other rooms within the home. It is the one place where wet, bare feet are expected, and water splashes on the walls are inevitable. This means that design preferences have to be balanced with practical considerations.

If you are thinking of using wallpapers, then solid vinyl is a must as it has a thick polymer coating that acts as a barrier to water penetration. However, vinyl is not suitable for use around showers, and it is best avoided around the bath – use an impervious product instead.

Paints are a good option, and manufacturers are now producing mildew- and water-resistant products especially for use in kitchens and bathrooms. Plain painted walls in vivid colors can produce the best contemporary styles, while gentle decorative paint finishes can add a softness or texture to the most imaginative of color schemes. Paint can also be used for stencilling, a simple way of adding pattern to a room.

Ceramic, slate and marble tiles offer the most versatile and practical finishes for the bathroom and they are suitable for wall and floor coverings, both in and out of the shower. Be cautious, however, as some highly glazed products are slippery underfoot when wet. There is a design of ceramic

THE SIMPLE THINGS
◀ Ceramic tiles give pattern and texture to a room and, when installed correctly, are totally impervious to moisture.

PAINT EFFECTS
▼ Paint is a most versatile product. It can be used to just add color or, as here, to produce the most effective of fantasy finishes.

tile to suit all styles of decor: beautifully detailed Victorian designs, rustic hand-pressed terracotta, and literally thousands of plain tiles with borders and decorative accents.

When considering the decor of a bathroom, think beyond the obvious. Mirrors, for example, can add an interesting perspective, and glass block walls and partitions are also very effective,

GLASS BLOCKS
Ceramic tiles are an obvious choice when decorating bathrooms, but it is sometimes nice to think beyond the more usual and employ items like glass blocks, creating a wall full of light and texture.

NATURE'S OWN
Natural wood and floor coverings team together here to produce a warm, textured room.

adding design detail without pattern. Likewise, wood has a natural beauty that can enhance a room, adding warmth and texture. Many color schemes now include stained and colorwashed or distressed wood walls and floors. These finishes make timber very versatile as they give many more design options. And with the availability of quality varnish sealants, most wood can now

be used around the tub and sink, without concern for warping or distortion.

Many people use carpets and, more recently, natural coir or sisal floor coverings in the bathroom. Many people have no problems with using one of these products in the bathroom or powder room. However, they can cause problems if they become wet, quite often giving off a damp odor and, in some cases, rotting. If you like the feel of carpet underfoot, why not invest in a specially manufactured carpet that repels most water splashes, or look for a rug which can be positioned away from areas prone to water splashes.

PRACTICAL TILES
▲ Floors should be washable and practical and, using two colors of floor tiles, can add pattern and a new dimension to a scheme.

TONGUE AND GROOVE
◀ Paint can be used to add a new look to wood, making this natural product extremely versatile. Use an eggshell or semi-gloss finish, or varnish your woodwork if you are concerned it will not endure the rigors of daily use.

Mirrors *and* sinks

One of the areas in the bathroom that can provide dramatic impact is around the wash sink. Teamed with a mirror, it provides a focal point, which you can have great fun accessorizing.

The type of vanity unit or sink you choose very much sets the style for the room. A simple, modern white sink adopts a number of different characters depending on the mirror and accessories you team with it. Pastel accessories and a pretty, intricate mirror will give a feminine touch, whereas a large, ornate mirror will create a more formal, classical look. A large gilt mirror positioned above an elegant twin sink vanity unit will not only reflect light into the room, but also enhances that well-decorated look, synonymous with town house interiors.

When trying to reproduce a certain style of decor, you should never restrict yourself to the usual products that are available. Instead, reap dividends by applying a little ingenuity and imagination: a

CLARITY
◀ Modern sinks are available in smooth, clean lines.

REFLECTIONS
▼ With its surrounding wall-mounted lights, heavy gilt mirror and pin-striped wallpaper, this sink area is reminiscent of early French splendor. Notice the clear plastic panel protecting the wallpaper from splashes.

TWIN SINKS
▲ A double vanity unit topped with white marble and gilt fittings set the scene for the large gilt mirror above. Vanity units have plenty of room to display pots, bottles and potions as well as vases of flowers for a more feminine touch.

rustic, country-style bathroom would not benefit from a simple modern sink by itself; yet house it in an old pine chest or Victorian washstand and it would sit perfectly alongside rough plastered walls and a flagstone floor. Think about using furniture not usually associated with bathrooms. Old ice boxes provide unusual storage space; add chairs, sofas (if you have the space) and soft furnishings. Just remember that any wooden surfaces that are likely to get wet should be protected from accidental spillages with varnish or a sheet of clear rigid plastic.

OLD-FASHIONED VANITY
▶ A large rustic pine chest is an unusual but very effective home for a standard white sink. It also provides ample storage for towels and other bathroom paraphernalia.

Window *treatments*

The style of window treatment you choose should depend on the style and size of your bathroom. Larger rooms tend to have less ventilation problems and therefore don't suffer from condensation. If this is the case, simply choose a window treatment that enhances the chosen style of your room. Anything from swags and tails to the simplest blinds can look marvellous.

If you have a small bathroom, it is always best to keep things simple or practical. Roman blinds are one of the least complicated forms of fabric blind available, as are roller or even tie-up blinds. Any of these can be made from virtually any fabric you like and are simple to remove for cleaning.

SHUT IT OUT
▲ Venetian blinds are delightfully simple in style and to attach to a window. They are available ready-made in a range of different widths and colors.

SOFT AND PRETTY
Lace gives a romantic feel to a room. If you changed the window treatment used here to a simple fabric Roman blind, for example, the scheme would still work. But it would have a more formal ambience.

Likewise, lace can add a romantic air to a room. As well as the vast range of cotton laces available, there are also a number of synthetic lace designs that have the look of cotton, and don't have that shiny quality found in most synthetic fiber laces. Such fabrics are ideal for the bathroom as you will find that they are mostly resistant to mildew growth.

Fabric curtains and blinds apart, consider installing a wooden blind or shutter system. Vertical and Venetian blinds are simple and effective. Wooden shutters, too, are becoming popular and they can be finished in a number of different ways such as distressing, staining or just plain painting.

SWINGING SHUTTERS
▲ Wooden shutters have a European feel, adding a chic simplicity to a window.

SIMPLICITY
The Roman blind is one of the most versatile of window treatments. It works in most settings and in most fabrics. This treatment is particularly effective when linkng two windows of different sizes.

Fixtures

There are many styles of bathroom fixtures now available. Here, we look at a number of the more readily available options. Bathtubs come in a number of different materials, styles and colors, the most hard-wearing of which is the cast-iron or steel, enamelled bathtub. It is quite heavy and more expensive than its acrylic cousins, but for durability it is second to none. Its only drawback is that it is prone to chipping.

Acrylic bathtubs are lighter, normally cheaper, and come in a larger range of colors than the traditional cast-iron bath. Another feature that many find attractive is that acrylic baths are warm to the touch. Glass-reinforced polyester bathtubs are also available. This material is far more rigid than acrylic and lends itself to certain tub styles, such as the free-standing, reproduction, claw-footed tub.

Showers are more economical to use than tubs and can be installed either above a bathtub or in their own cubicles. There is a large range of styles: anything from the traditional, large-headed chrome shower to the ultra-modern power showers.

Sinks are made in the form of a sink resting on a pedestal or designed to fit into a vanity unit, which would, in turn, offer additional storage. Both types are available in a suitably wide selection of styles and colors.

Most toilets are manufactured from vitreous

RUNNING HOT AND COLD
◀ Designers are taking more and more time in creating bathroom fixtures. Practicality now goes hand in hand with good styling.

SPACE SAVING
▼ The area below a sink on a pedestal is a waste of good space. With vanity units, this area is used in a practical way, making added storage.

china and, once again, come in many colors and styles. They also come in various heights, and with different flushing mechanisms, which should be taken into consideration before you purchase.

Bath and sink faucets should be easy to handle and direct the water into the unit proficiently. Faucets can be fixed to the wall or mounted onto the bath, sink, or vanity unit. The range of styles is breathtaking; everything from the sophisticated mixer unit with shower, available in both contemporary and reproductions styles, to the chrome/gold fixtures.

NEW FOR OLD
▲ Many technological advances are being made in the bathroom. This hydroshower is one of the latest, containing water massage jets down the sides and an overhead shower producing either a strong water-flow for a stimulating massage or a gentle, pleasant and relaxing vaporized water-flow.

CORNERED
▲ Corner units can take up an area within a room which otherwise might be wasted.

Space saving
and storage

Many modern houses and apartments are now quite small, leaving a bathroom with very limited space. In small rooms, space-saving tricks and well-thought-out storage are two keys to success. For example, scaled down tubs and sinks are available, but they can be uncomfortable to use, so look for corner tubs and vanity units. These can give you a full sink or tub positioned into an otherwise unusable space.

Many rooms are dormer-style, with sloping ceilings that are hard to decorate. Building a shower unit where there is maximum height and utilizing the remaining space for storage is one

OPEN PLAN
▶ Custom-built open shelves add storage and a decorative element to a room. Colored towels can be used to blend in with or add contrast to a bathroom.

SEPARATION

▶ By separating a shower from the main room, the space will look less cluttered and also larger.

idea. However, if you decide to place a toilet in such an area, make sure there is ample headroom in front of it as well as directly above. Alternatively, consider incorporating a shower into your bedroom if the family bathroom lacks space.

Storage is always a consideration in the bathroom, regardless of its size, and different styles of room require different storage solutions. Metal chrome shelves look wonderful in a modern bathroom, while traditional, freestanding pieces of antique furniture are often the perfect solution in a period setting. Don't be afraid to take the creative approach and adapt pieces of furniture to suit the room. A verdigris paint finish on a new piece of furniture can transform it into a prized piece for the most traditional of rooms.

Most items stored in the bathroom are quite small, and can be housed easily on shelves and in small cabinets. A bath rack is

SPACE SAVER
▲ This colorful shower is built into the eaves of the house, with a window in the roof to add light. You could fit either a curtain or a door on the front for greater privacy or to prevent water from spilling onto the carpet.

MADE-TO-MEASURE
◄ Maximum bathroom storage is achieved by using custom-built units.

HIDING AWAY
A simple curtain can hide all the plumbing, potions and lotions that are found in virtually every bathroom.

one solution for accessories when space is at a premium within the room. And if you are creating boxing for a bath or pipes, incorporate recessed shelving or neat cabinets into the structure. For a softer finish to open shelves, add curtains that can be simply attached with narrow rails beneath a shelf or edge of the vanity unit, such as in the picture featured above.

Bathrooms are now starting to receive similar treatment to kitchens, with many manufacturers producing custom-made cabinets for use with certain styles of fixtures. This means that maximum use is made of the space available, and a streamlined look is given to the room.

Practical *and* safe

Apart from the kitchen, the bathroom can be a most hazardous place and it is very important to bear this in mind when planning, decorating or using your bathroom.

However wonderful a shiny, tiled or marble floor may look, it is not always practical, so ensure that floor tiles are specially designed to have a non-slip surface. Make sure that shower screens and glass doors are shatterproof and that any mirrors are securely attached to the wall. As water and electricity do not mix, you must adhere to electrical regulations. Enclose all electrical lights, to ensure that no moisture can penetrate and short-circuit the system, and either position light switches outside the room or replace them with a special pull-cord system. And never trail a connected electrical appliance, such as a hairdryer, into the bathroom.

As we frequently keep disinfectants and chemical cleaners in the bathroom, store them in a secure cabinet out of the reach of children, together with all medicines and vitamin supplements.

In a family bathroom, ensure there are no shelves above the bath that may encourage a curious child to climb. Accessories such as toothbrush holders should be made of plastic and if small children or elderly people are using the bath, provide an anti-slip mat and rails. Most importantly, never let a young child use a bathroom unattended.

TEMPERATURE GAUGE
Mixer faucets are useful – particularly for children – to establish the correct water temperature when washing.

MAINTAINING SAFETY IN THE
BATHROOM

• Never use an electric heater in the bathroom unless it is an especially adapted, wall-mounted one.

• Never use a hairdryer or other electrical appliance in a bathroom by plugging it into a neighboring room or on an extension lead.

• Keep chemical cleaners and all medicines well out of reach of children. Medicines should be in a lockable cabinet. Do not site them above the toilet as children automatically use this to stand on.

• Ensure flooring is non-slippery. Any rugs should have anti-slip matting beneath them.

• Electrical switches and sockets (with the exception of a shaving point) should be sited outside the bathroom.

• Elderly people and young children will probably need an anti-slip mat and rails in the bath to prevent accidents.

• Regularly check baths and showers for leakages. These need to be caught early. Often, it is a simple matter of resealing edges with a bath sealant.

• Ensure the bathroom has adequate ventilation. Condensation build-up will cause mildew, discoloration and deterioration of wood, and eventually plasterwork.

Acknowledgments

The author and publishers would like to thank the following companies and their PR agencies for the loan of photographs and props used in this book

Alternative Plans: page 34l, 66t
Czech & Speake: page 6t, 7
Crown Paints: page 65;
Crucial Trading page 12b;
Cardon Bathrooms Ltd page 12t, 19t, 24, 25,29, 30, 47t, 58, 74b
Descamp: page 31b
Doulton: page 32, 53
Dulux: page 15, 33b, 34-35, 47b
English Stamp Company: page 25t
Faral Radiators: page 39t
Habitat: page 35t
Ideal Standard: page 9b, 61, 70t
Mira Showers: page 37, 50, 56, 73, 74t
The Pier: page 31t, 48t
Pret a Vivre: page 17
Samuel Heath and Sons: page 17t, 71t
Stiebel of Nottingham: page 22
Teuco: pages 4-5, 19b, 39b, 71b;
Trent bathrooms: page 44
V V Rouleux tassels: page 17:
Vernon Tutbury: page 69, 72
Winchester Tiles: page 106

Picture Credits
Elizabeth Whiting Associates: title page, 10, 11t (r & l), 18, 40, 43, 45, 54, 55t, 62t&b; 63, 70b, 72b, 75;
Abode: page 11bl, 13, 16, 33t, 47, 49, 68
Lizzie Orme: page 20
Paul Ryan/International Interiors: page 11br, 23, 27b, 38, 55b, 66b, 67t&b
Ashley Morrison: page 26b, 7t; 60
Jon Bouchier: page 64

Index